1.

SPORTS SUPERSTARS
ALEXIA PUTELLAS

BY GOLRIZ GOLKAR

BELLWETHER MEDIA • MINNEAPOLIS, MN

Torque brims with excitement perfect for thrill-seekers of all kinds. Discover daring survival skills, explore uncharted worlds, and marvel at mighty engines and extreme sports. In *Torque* books, anything can happen. Are you ready?

This edition first published in 2025 by Bellwether Media, Inc.

No part of this publication may be reproduced in whole or in part without written permission of the publisher. For information regarding permission, write to Bellwether Media, Inc., Attention: Permissions Department, 6012 Blue Circle Drive, Minnetonka, MN 55343.

Library of Congress Cataloging-in-Publication Data

Names: Golkar, Golriz, author.
Title: Alexia Putellas / by Golriz Golkar.
Description: Minneapolis, MN : Bellwether Media, 2025. | Series: Sports superstars | Includes bibliographical references and index. | Audience: Ages 7-12 | Audience: Grades 4-6 | Summary: "Engaging images accompany information about Alexia Putellas. The combination of high-interest subject matter and light text is intended for students in grades 3 through 7"– Provided by publisher.
Identifiers: LCCN 2024009921 (print) | LCCN 2024009922 (ebook) | ISBN 9798893040333 (library binding) | ISBN 9781644879696 (ebook)
Subjects: LCSH: Putellas, Alexia–Juvenile literature. | Women soccer players–Spain–Biography–Juvenile literature. | Soccer players–Spain–Biographpy–Juvenile literature.
Classification: LCC GV942.7.P88 G65 2025 (print) | LCC GV942.7.P88 (ebook) | DDC 796.334092 [B]–dc23/eng/20240402
LC record available at https://lccn.loc.gov/2024009921
LC ebook record available at https://lccn.loc.gov/2024009922

Text copyright © 2025 by Bellwether Media, Inc. TORQUE and associated logos are trademarks and/or registered trademarks of Bellwether Media, Inc. Bellwether Media is a division of Chrysalis Education Group.

Editor: Kieran Downs   Designer: Gabriel Hilger

Printed in the United States of America, North Mankato, MN.

TABLE OF CONTENTS

A GREAT PASS	4
WHO IS ALEXIA PUTELLAS?	6
A RISING SOCCER STAR	8
SOCCER SUPERSTAR	12
PUTELLAS'S FUTURE	20
GLOSSARY	22
TO LEARN MORE	23
INDEX	24

A GREAT PASS

It is the 2023 **Women's World Cup**. Spain is playing Zambia. Alexia Putellas takes the ball for Spain. She looks for an open teammate.

Putellas passes the ball high in the air. Her teammate hits it with her head. Spain scores! They go on to win the match 5–0.

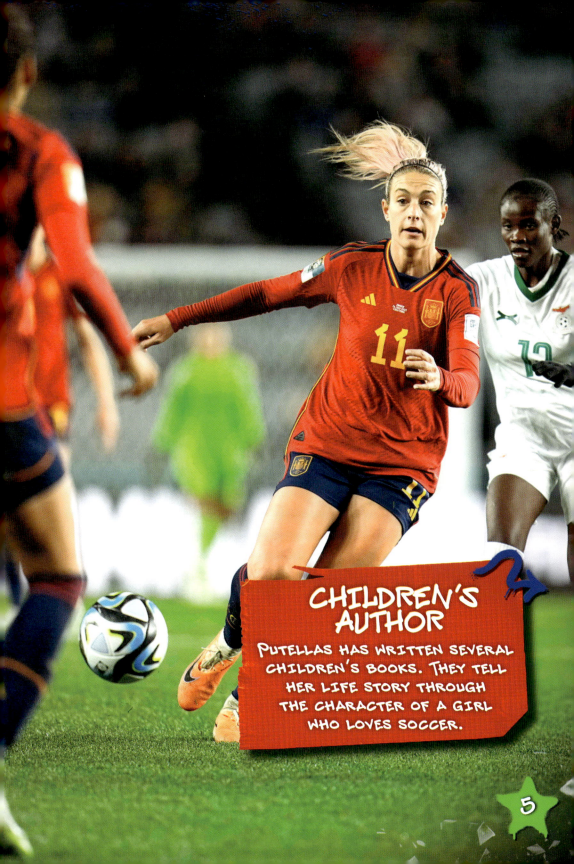

CHILDREN'S AUTHOR

Putellas has written several children's books. They tell her life story through the character of a girl who loves soccer.

WHO IS ALEXIA PUTELLAS?

Alexia Putellas is a soccer player. She plays **midfield** for FC Barcelona. She also plays for Spain's national team. She has won every major European club and individual soccer award.

SOCCER DREAMS

Spain did not always have paid women's soccer teams. Putellas went to college to study business. She left school when paid teams were formed.

ALEXIA PUTELLAS

BIRTHDAY February 4, 1994

HOMETOWN Mollet del Vallès, Spain

POSITION midfield

HEIGHT 5 feet 7 inches

JOINED Espanyol in 2010

Putellas is also a businesswoman. She works with companies that make sports products. She also works for **gender equality** in women's sports.

A RISING SOCCER STAR

Putellas started playing on soccer teams at age 7. She first joined the Sabadell youth club. At age 10, she joined La Masia **academy**. She trained with other young players for the FC Barcelona team.

LA MASIA

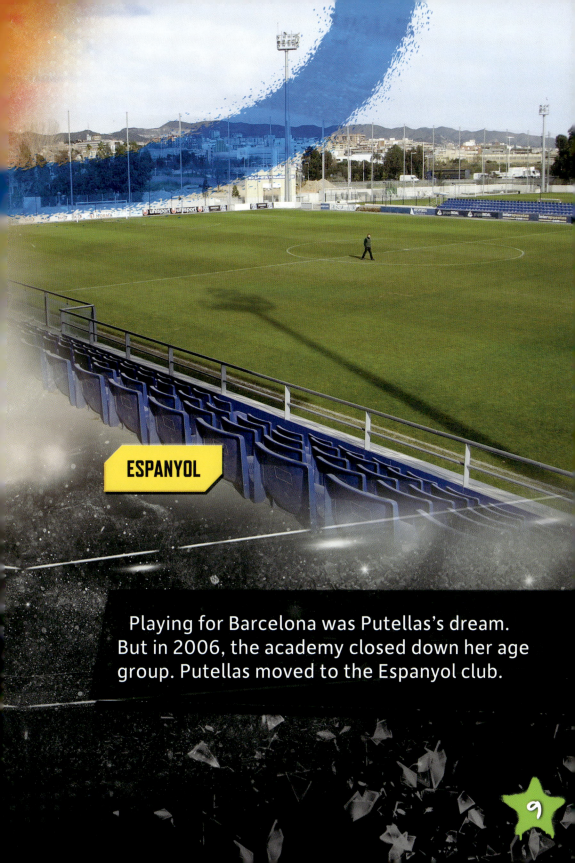

ESPANYOL

Playing for Barcelona was Putellas's dream. But in 2006, the academy closed down her age group. Putellas moved to the Espanyol club.

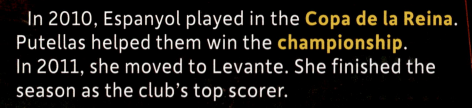

In 2010, Espanyol played in the **Copa de la Reina**. Putellas helped them win the **championship**. In 2011, she moved to Levante. She finished the season as the club's top scorer.

Putellas also played for the Spanish national team. She helped them win the **UEFA** Women's U-17 championship in 2010 and 2011.

2010 COPA DE LA REINA

FAVORITES

SINGER	FOOD	PET	SOCCER PLAYER

Beyoncé	Japanese food	dogs	Louisa Nécib

FATHERLY LOVE

Putellas's father supported her soccer dreams. He went to her games even when he was sick. Since his passing, Putellas points to the sky before every game to honor him.

SOCCER SUPERSTAR

Putellas finally joined FC Barcelona in 2012. In 2013, she helped her team win the **league** title. She also helped the team win the Copa de la Reina. She was named **Most Valuable Player** (MVP) of the finals.

In 2014, they won the Copa de la Reina again. She was MVP again!

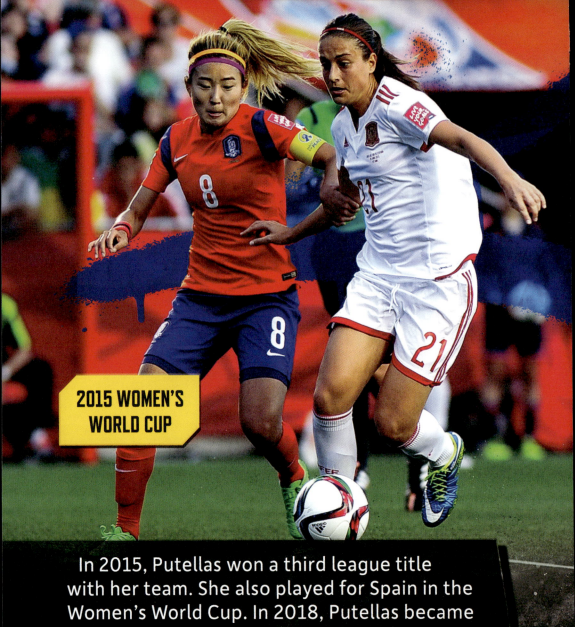

2015 WOMEN'S WORLD CUP

In 2015, Putellas won a third league title with her team. She also played for Spain in the Women's World Cup. In 2018, Putellas became one of Barcelona's captains.

Putellas played for Spain again in the 2019 World Cup. She helped Barcelona win the 2020 Copa de la Reina. She also helped Barcelona win the first Women's Spanish **Supercopa**.

ALEXIA PUTELLAS MAP

- RCD Espaynol, Sant Adrià de Besòs, Spain — 2006 to 2011
- Levante UD, Buñol, Spain — 2011 to 2012
- FC Barcelona, Barcelona, Spain — 2012 to present

2020 COPA DE LA REINA

In 2021, Putellas led Barcelona to the **Women's Champions League** title. She also won her first **Ballon d'Or**. She was named the UEFA Women's Player of the Year. She also won the Best **FIFA** Women's Player.

Putellas also helped Barcelona win another Copa de la Reina. She became the first player to be named finals MVP three times.

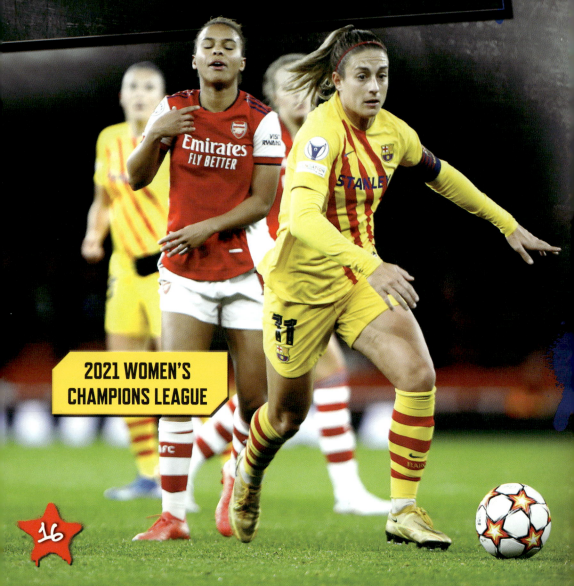

2021 WOMEN'S CHAMPIONS LEAGUE

BACK-TO-BACK

Putellas won the Ballon d'Or, Best FIFA Women's Player, and UEFA Women's Player of the Year two years in a row. She is the first player to do so!*

2021 BALLON D'OR

TROPHY SHELF

FIFA Women's World Cup champion

2-time Best FIFA Women's Player

2-time Ballon d'Or winner

2-time UEFA Women's Player of the Year

8-time Copa de la Reina champion

17

Putellas won her second Ballon d'Or for the 2021–2022 season. She also won the Best FIFA Women's Player again.

In 2022, Putellas hurt her leg. She could not play for a year. Putellas's leg healed in time to win another league title with FC Barcelona in 2023. She also helped Spain win their first Women's World Cup in 2023.

2022 BALLON D'OR

TIMELINE

— 2006 —
Putellas joins Espanyol

— 2011 —
Putellas joins Levante

— 2012 —
Putellas joins FC Barcelona

100 GAMES

In 2022, Putellas became the first Spanish women's soccer player to play in 100 games for her country.

— 2018 —
Putellas becomes a team captain

— 2021 —
Putellas wins her first Ballon d'Or

— 2023 —
Spain wins the FIFA Women's World Cup

PUTELLAS'S FUTURE

Off the field, Putellas fights for equality in women's sports. She works with groups that help spread women's sports. She wants women to be treated and paid fairly.

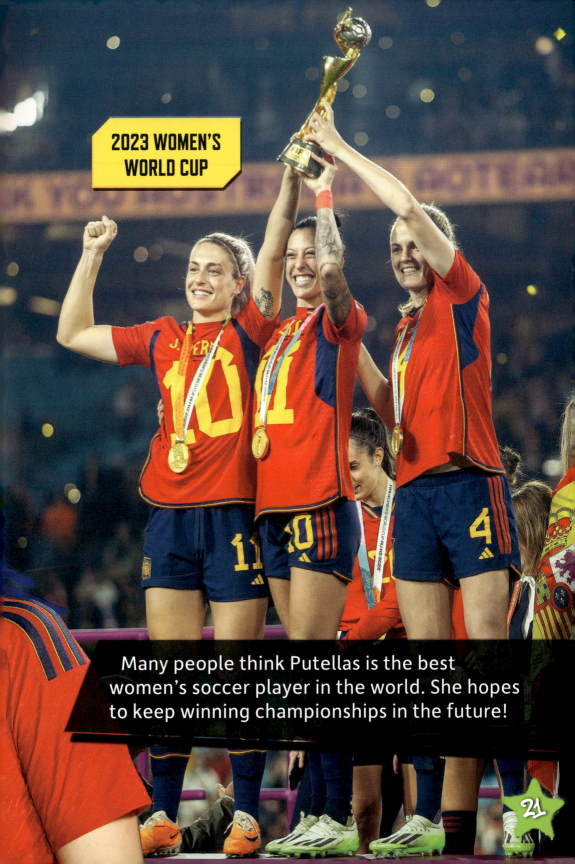

2023 WOMEN'S WORLD CUP

Many people think Putellas is the best women's soccer player in the world. She hopes to keep winning championships in the future!

GLOSSARY

academy—a school that teaches a certain subject

Ballon d'Or—an annual soccer award given to the best male and female player of the year

championship—a contest to decide the best team or person

Copa de la Reina—the championship tournament for professional women's soccer in Spain

FIFA—Fédération Internationale de Football Association; FIFA is an international association that oversees soccer and two other related sports.

gender equality—when rights or opportunities are not affected by which gender a person uses to identify themselves

league—a group of sports teams that often play against one another

midfield—a player in soccer who covers most of the field

most valuable player—the best player in a year, game, or series; the most valuable player is often called the MVP.

Supercopa—a soccer tournament in Spain in which winners and runners-up from other Spanish tournaments play against each other

UEFA—Union of European Football Associations; UEFA controls soccer in Europe.

Women's Champions League—a European women's soccer tournament where the winners of the top European leagues play each other to decide the best team in Europe

Women's World Cup—an international soccer competition held every four years; the Women's World Cup is the world's largest women's soccer tournament.

TO LEARN MORE

AT THE LIBRARY

Bolte, Mari. *FIFA*. North Mankato, Minn.: Norwood House Press, 2023.

Golkar, Golriz. *Megan Rapinoe*. Minneapolis, Minn.: Bellwether Media, 2024.

Shaw, Gina. *What Is the Women's World Cup?* New York, N.Y.: Penguin Workshop, 2023.

ON THE WEB

Factsurfer.com gives you a safe, fun way to find more information.

1. Go to www.factsurfer.com

2. Enter "Alexia Putellas" into the search box and click 🔍.

3. Select your book cover to see a list of related content.

INDEX

awards, 6, 12, 13, 16, 17, 18
books, 5
business, 6, 7
captain, 14
championship, 10, 12, 14, 16, 21
childhood, 8, 9, 10
college, 6
Copa de la Reina, 10, 12, 13, 14, 15, 16
equality, 7, 20
Espanyol, 9, 10
family, 11
favorites, 11
FC Barcelona, 6, 8, 9, 12, 14, 16, 18
future, 21
games, 19
hurt, 18
La Masia, 8, 9
Levante, 10
map, 15
midfield, 6
most valuable player, 12, 13, 16
profile, 7
Sabadell, 8
Spain, 4, 6, 10, 14, 18, 19
timeline, 18–19
trophy shelf, 17
Women's Champions League, 16
Women's Spanish Supercopa, 14
Women's World Cup, 4, 14, 18, 21

The images in this book are reproduced through the courtesy of: Sportimage Ltd/ Alamy, front cover; Christian Bertrand, pp. 3, 7, (Alexia Putellas), 23; Abbie Parr/ AP Images, p. 4; Cal Sport Media/ Alamy, pp. 4-5; PRESSINPHOTO SPORTS AGENCY/ Alamy, pp. 6-7; charnsitr, p. 7 (logo); Matthew Ashton/ Contributor/ Getty, p. 8; No Source/ Wikipedia, pp. 9, 15 (Espaynol); Sr Mou/ Wikipedia, p. 10; CRIS BOURONCLE/ Getty, p. 11; Suzan Moore/ Alamy, p. 11 (Beyoncé); Caito, p. 11 (Japanese food); Viorel Sima, p. 11 (dogs); Aflo Co. Ltd./ Alamy, p. 11 (Louisa Nécib); MAJA SUSLIN/ AP Images, p. 12; Matej Divizna/ Contributor/ Getty, p. 13; Steven Kingsman/ AP Images, p. 14; ESPA Photo Agency/ AP Images, p. 15; Wilnel José Vernú Guerrero/ Wikipedia, p. 15 (Barcelona); Levante Unión Deportiva/ Wikipedia, p. 15 (Levante); NurPhoto SRL/ Alamy, p. 16; Px Images/ Alamy, p. 17; Francois Mori/ AP Images, p. 18 (2022 Ballon d'Or); RCD Espanyol/ Wikipedia, p. 18 (Espanyol Logo); Levante Unión Deportiva/ Wikipedia, p. 18 (Levante Logo); FC Barcelona/ Wikipedia, p. 18 (FC Barcelona Logo); ZUMA Press, Inc./ Alamy, pp. 18-19, 21; Xinhua/ Alamy, p. 19 (2021); Speed Media/ Icon Sportswire/ AP Images, p. 20.